IMAGES OF ENGLAND

LISKEARD

Liskeard & District Choral Society

Founded 1869

President: ERNEST GIBSON ESQ.

THURSDAY
MARCH 24th
1949

CONCERT

SOLOISTS:

ANNE ZIEGLER

AND

WEBSTER BOOTH

Conductor: PERCIVAL C. W. HILL

PROGRAMME 6D.

Musical concerts in Liskeard were always popular, none more so than in 1949 when Anne Zeigler and Webster Booth came to the town as guests of the Liskeard and District Choral Society who performed under the baton of Mr Percival Hill. Note the famous autographs on the programme cover.

IMAGES OF ENGLAND

LISKEARD

JOHN NEALE

The
History
Press

The crest of the Ancient Borough of Liskeard.

For Douglas Lewis, 1918–2005, a dear Liskeard friend, to whom I owe everything...
a debt which can never be amply repaid.

First published in 1998 by The Chalford Publishing Company

Reprinted in 2010 by
The History Press
The Mill, Brimscombe Port,
Stroud, Gloucestershire, GL5 2QG
www.thehistorypress.co.uk

Reprinted in 2011

British Library Cataloguing in Publication Data.
A catalogue record for this book is available from the British Library.

ISBN 978 0 7524 1034 0

Typesetting and origination by The Chalford Publishing Company.
Printed and bound in England.

An early illustration of Liskeard by Samuel Prout, (1783-1852). He specialised in romantic views of English towns, villages and landscapes.

Contents

The drinking fountain on the Parade.

Acknowledgements

I should like to thank the following people and organisations who have generously provided photographs and freely given information for this book.

Mrs E. Borlase, Mrs M. Bunt, Mrs M. Bartlett, Miss A.Clark, Mrs M.Cayzer, Miss V.Cayzer, Mr P. Cowling, Coath of Liskeard, Mrs K. Davy, Mr M. Davey, Mr and Mrs W.P. Doney, Mrs S.Gale, Mr and Mrs W.N. Gale, Mr A.Gwillam, Mrs P. Hodge, Mr and Mrs J. Hoskins, Mr W. Hoskin for all his interest and help, Mr and Mrs J. Howarth, Ms Liz Harrington, Mr and Mrs D. Harris, Mr G. Huddy, Mrs G. Killingly, Mr D. Lewis, Miss Y. Lewis, Miss J. Lock, Mrs M. McGowan, Miss M. Marrack, Mr and Mrs A. Masters, Mrs J. Morris, Mrs B. Millman, Mr T. Marshall, Mrs J. Mann, Mrs L.Olver, Mr and Mr N. Pampling, Mrs J. Pengelly, Mr Ray Roberts, Mrs H. Searle, Mrs H. Sharpe, Mrs M.Tozer, Mrs C. Thompson, Mrs Thomas, (St Neot History Group) Miss P. Tucker, Mr and Mrs Ugalde, Mrs A.Webster, Mr and Mrs D. Warring, Mr and Mrs P. Warring, Mrs S. Williams, Mrs R. Wilton, Jon Wooldridge.

Special thanks are due to Friths, Argall, Valentine, Overland, Botterell and other anonymous publishers for the use of picture postcards from their collections. To Mr John Rapson and Mr David Hambly (Photography Liskeard) for particular photographs. The Cornish Times, Liskeard, The Cornish Guardian, Bodmin for use of their files. To John Allen, Mr Peter Moore, Mr Martin Lister, and Mr Bernard Deacon for 'pointers' contained in the pages of their books on Liskeard. To Mr Terry Knight and Miss Kim Cooper, Local Studies Library, Redruth. The librarians and staff of the Cornwall County Branch Libraries at Liskeard, Bodmin and Launceston who all answered questions with patience and courtesy. To Mr Mark Quick and staff of 'Quick Print' Launceston who worked miracles on seemingly impossible photographs and to all those photographers of yesterday who failed to sign their work but whose pictures helped to make this volume possible.

Apologies are due to anyone whom I have inadvertently overlooked.

Introduction

There is one important point to be made about this book from the outset. It is not in any way intended to be a history of Liskeard. That mammoth task has been undertaken and written by far worthier men than myself. This volume is an exploration: a mosaic of people, events, scenes, places and happenings in the town and district coupled with snippets of historical fact and half forgotten memories and perhaps the glimpse of a dear face, sadly no longer with us. The character of Liskeard is fiercely Cornish and independent and long may it remain so. Fortunately the town is just far enough away from the River Tamar, for much of its length Cornwall's natural boundary, not to be over-shadowed by or afraid of being swallowed up by Plymouth, its nearest Devonian neighbour.

The exact age of Liskeard is lost in the avenues of years but one thing is certain, there was a settlement here from earliest times. One of the first mentions of Liskeard comes in AD 1000 when it was called Lyscerryt; by the time the Domesday Book was compiled it had become Liscarrot then variously Lyskerret, Lescars, Lyscard and in 1600 Liskeard.

Liskeard's first Charter, one of the earliest to be granted to any town in the country dates from 1240 and was presented to the town by Richard Earl of Cornwall and brother of King Henry III. So by this time, way over 750 years ago, Liskeard was a place of some considerable standing. Another charter dating from 1266 gives Liskeard permission to hold two fairs: one at the Assumption of the Blessed Virgin Mary and the other at the Feast of St Matthew the Apostle and Evangelist. Liskeard also returned two Members to Parliament from 1294-1832.

In the hey-day of coach travel Liskeard was an important stopping point on the route through Cornwall from Torpoint to Falmouth, and at one time there were a number of coaching inns in the town.

One of the first major changes to affect Liskeard was the opening in 1825 of the Looe to Liskeard canal. This six mile long waterway with numerous locks from Tarras Pill by Looe to Moorswater below Liskeard, ensured that modest prosperity came to the town as farm produce and later, copper and tin, could be more easily transported to the coast, and sea sand for use on the farms and coal brought up to Liskeard.

During the late nineteenth century Liskeard, prospered and grew considerably, due to two important events both of which were to have long lasting effects on the area: the discovery of rich lodes of copper and tin round the Caradon Hill area, giving rise to several close-knit moorland communities and the arrival of the Great Western Railway. Consequently after the mineral discoveries Liskeard became an important centre for the coining and taxing of tin being one of the Cornish Stannary towns. One hundred years later with much of the mineral wealth exhausted, one by one the mines closed and now only the blind-eyed engine houses remain.

The hub of a mainly agricultural area, Liskeard developed into one of the largest twice weekly markets in the district; the local farmers and their wives still come to market just as their forebears did all those years ago.

Liskeard means different things to different people. For some it is home; for others it represents the need for employment and for others who are nearer retirement age a place to which to return when they feel unable to resist further the pull of ancestral ties.

Local history in towns and villages is reflected in the daily lives of the ordinary people, so many changes have taken place during the course of one life time. Fashion, transport, types of employment communication of all kinds. Many businesses too have come and gone.

In a volume such as this the selection of illustrations has been very much a personal choice. Hopefully there will be something of interest for everyone.

I am not a native of Liskeard, so for me it has been a privilege afforded unreservedly by Liskeard residents who have allowed me to sift through their personal photographs, many of which depict less hurried days, a vanished way of life or a long gone event and to share in the memories some happy, others sad, which they evoke.

This small volume is a nostalgic look back over the shoulder to the Liskeard and district of yesterday and if it does nothing more than to persuade one person to rescue an album or even a single photograph instead of throwing them away, I will be well pleased, and this volume will have more than served its purpose.

John Neale, Launceston, 1998

A view from St Martin's church tower. The Market House is in the top centre of the picture.

One

Liskeard: The Town

The Parade, being the centre of Liskeard is probably the part of the town where the most noticeable changes have taken place…some drastic, others more subtle.

Currently, plans for further developments are on the board and the future of Webb's Hotel is in the balance. It is now Webb's House, Home of the *Cornish Times* Newspaper Offices. Elsewhere, over the years, in the side streets, buildings have been demolished to make way for road widening and visibility improvement: shops and shop fronts have come and gone and all have contributed to the overall change in the general street-scape.

A busy period on The Parade. It looks as if coaches have just arrived in the town. Guests are probably leaving or arriving at Webb's Hotel. In later years 'Webb's bus' used to meet every train and convey commercial travellers and other guests up from the station.

A view across the expanse of The Parade toward Barras Street and Trehawke House. On the left is Sweet's monumental masons yard and next door Middleton House, with Webb's Hotel just nosing into the scene. The present day post office occupies the site of Middleton House and a somewhat derelict garage that of the monumental mason.

Torrential rain sweeps across The Parade on a market day around the turn of the century. Agricultural implements, sheep and cattle from the local farms are being sold. Note the foliage shrouding the frontage of Parade House.

The north side of The Parade. The men and women seem fascinated by the camera and are quite happy to pose for the photographer.

Looking across The Parade and down Barras (Barrel) Street. It is interesting to see that motor vehicles have not completely ousted horse-drawn traffic. Prior to 1811 this view would have been impossible as houses and a public house stretched across The Parade and there were gardens where Webb's Hotel now stands. Trehawke House has been demolished.

There is one notable change in this scene of The Parade. Middleton House, built as a gentleman's residence in 1843, and at one time the home of the Beech family has been demolished. During the Second World War it was used as the Food Office, MAFF Office and ARP Office. Today the modern post office building of 1963 which some still find jarring, occupies the site.

The Parade in the late 1930s, looking toward Parade House, Barras Place and West Street, (Horns Lane). The view was probably photographed from Webb's Hotel, now Webb's House. Note the wide variety of cars of the time. The Fountain has been upgraded from an inn to a hotel, probably in an effort to keep step with Webb's on the opposite side.

The fashion in motor cars, Austin A40 Somerset and Standard Vanguard, can be seen in this view of The Parade from the entrance of Middleton House. The results of parliamentary elections were announced from the centre window of the building in the middle of the scene. Stone's restaurant was here too.

The Parade showing the Central Garage.

An early view of Barras Street and Stuart House, which was once the home of a prominent Liskeard Royalist, Joseph Jane. During the English Civil War, King Charles I lodged here before and after the Battle of Braddock Down, near Lostwithiel, in 1643.

THE LEY AND BARRAS STREET, LISKEARD.   96094. J.V.

The lower end of Barras Street where it joins Dean Street. The John Passmore Edwards Library, a gift to the town, is on the left and opposite, Taylor's Garage, which has disappeared, and beyond in Barn Street the frontage of the long vanished Temperance Hall is glimpsed. The Royal British Legion premises now occupy the site.

81350. LISKEARD, BARRAS STREET.

Looking up Barras Street sometime in the 1920s. The building in the right foreground, part of Stuart House, has been demolished. A bull-nosed Morris heads out of town.

Barras Street with the slate-hung Stuart House, minus its shroud of foliage and Trehawke House, once the home of John Allen who wrote, The History of Liskeard in 1857. Allen, a Quaker, lived here with his daughters.

Liskeard, Post Office, &c.

The junction of Barras Street, Dean Street, Windsor Place and Bay Tree Hill. The 'new post office' of 1911 on the left is now a shop selling greeting cards and Jago and Sons, established on the site of Trehawke House, became the National Provincial Bank in October 1954, which has in its turn given way to the National Westminster Bank.

DEAN STREET & NEW POST OFFICE, LISKEARD.

The east end of Dean Street soon after the turn of the century showing the 'new post office'. The Congregational Chapel, 1865, was demolished in 1964. Today a rest garden occupies the site where the houses on the left stand.

A deserted Dean Street, leading westward away from the town centre, the entrance to the Cattle Market is now on the left. Note the old street light outside the Albion Inn, now Fintan O'Malley's Irish café bar.

The Cattle Market established on the grounds of Trehawke House in the early 1900s, shown here in more recent times.

Dean Terrace in New Road on the way to Bodmin, was built by members of the Quaker community in the 1840s and was one of Liskeard's first Victorian terraces, then enjoying expansive views of the surrounding countryside.

The junction of Dean Terrace and Dean Hill.

New Road in the late 1920s. The road has not yet been surfaced with tarmacadam.

Liskeard's Wesleyan Chapel of 1841 in Barn Street was burned down after an arsonist's attack in June 1845. Two young men, Henry Lucas and Andrew Hingston, started a fund for the present chapel. The following September the foundation stones were laid and in June 1846 Dr Joseph Beaumont opened the Liskeard Wesleyan Chapel. Now, due to changes, the chapel is going to be known as Liskeard Methodist Church.

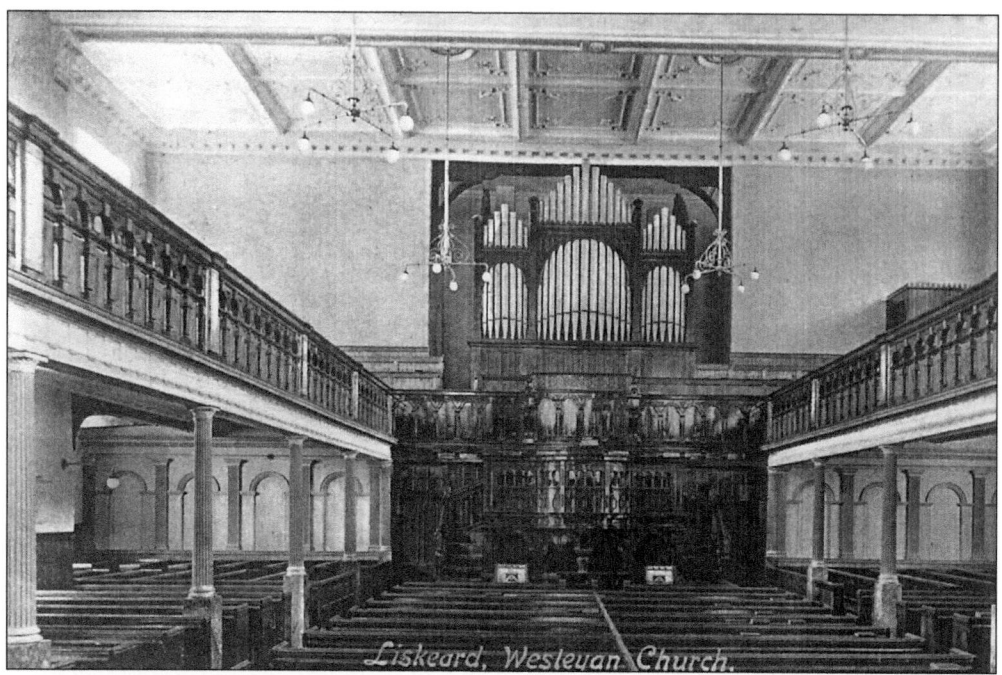

The spacious interior of the Wesleyan Chapel in the 1930s. The old gas lighting has now given way to electricity. Older people remember the resident caretaker who used to light the delicate chandelier gas lights, balancing precariously on a plank, using a long pole to reach the mantles. The organ too has been refurbished and the pulpit constructed by Ugalde's was given in memory of Dr Andrew Hingston.

The junction of Windsor Place and Barn Street with Chudleigh's butchers shop in its prominent position. It is now Town and Country Crafts. On the right is Bay Tree Hill and on the left, Dean Street corner.

Bay Tree Hill was once Liskeard's centre for badger baiting and in its season, Maypole dancing. In 1906 the Liberal Club was here and in more recent times a brewery run by Mr Daniel Venning; now Bay Tree Trading. The Talbot and Union Hotels were going concerns. Latterly Barnecutt's bakery, and James's dairy were here and on the extreme right, Selling's umbrella shop, long demolished.

The rear of the old brewery building in Bay Tree Hill and the backs of premises in Fore Street. This unusual view is from Sun Girt Lane. In the foreground are allotments and a glimpse of the Looe-Liskeard railway line and on the extreme right, the old church school.

Fore street, still a main shopping area of the town, shown here in the early 1900s.

Above, left: Little seems to have changed in this view of Fore Street apart from the fashions in clothes of both men and women.

Above, right: Maggs drapers and outfitters 'The Store' in Fore Street occupied the corner site with Bay Tree Hill. Older people still recall it fondly. Opposite was Cowling's newsagent, tobacconist and fancy goods emporium which was demolished to make way for Woolworth's. Here too was Ugalde's carpenters and furnishers.

Right: Another view of busy Fore Street.

Rayner's café and the Star Supply Stores which was rebuilt in 1961 and became the SWEB shop. The Blue Door café is also fondly remembered.

Opposite: Pike Street, probably in the 1950s. All the buildings in the left foreground have been demolished.

Left: A view of Pike Street, originally Tavern Hill, which probably dates from the 1940s. The advertising sign would seem to indicate that 'Tulip Wool' was all the rage. On the right is the Foresters Hall of 1896 and the shop front of Pipers drapers and outfitters. Right: Looking down steep Pike Street towards Market Street. On the right is the Guild Hall tower and the clock which was given by John Isaac, a coal merchant in the town. Beyond, the round frontage of the Market House is glimpsed and also seen is the exterior of 'Ough's', for over a hundred years one of Liskeard's leading grocers and chemists. The White Hart Hotel is on the left.

Liskeard, Pipe Well.

The Pipe Well, also known as St Martin's Well or the Well of Liskerret. This is one of the towns oldest sources of water supply. It is fed by four springs and said never to have run dry. The gates were added in 1879.

Market Street in the 1930s, with the Constitutional Club of 1911 on the right and in the centre is the Market House. Pickles Electric Cinema was on the first floor, closed soon after the Cinedrome, owned by the Pope Brothers opened. The boards advertising the current film and forthcoming attractions are seen outside. Note Stephen's Ink thermometer on the left. The car parked in the narrowest part of the street proves there were no traffic wardens in those days.

Market Street, Liskeard

A view of Market Street probably in the early 1900s as the Constitutional Club has yet to be built. The old horse appears to be waiting patiently while the men pass the time of day. At one time these premises were Chalice butchers shop.

Left: The semi-circular facade of the Market House built in 1822 for around £800. The building was finally demolished in 1956. Boots the chemist later occupied the site. Right: Going… going…gone. The Market House site in 1957.

Number 18 Church Street, known as the Ancient House, is probably the oldest inhabited dwelling in Liskeard. Since this picture was taken in about 1906 the granite steps adjoining the porch and the small building next door, once a barbers shop, have been removed. Today the ancient house is no longer slate-hung. It is still a private dwelling.

After extensive cracks, clearly seen in this photograph, appeared in St Martin's Church tower, it was shored up for several years. Discussions ensued as to whether it was best to restore the tower or demolish it and rebuild. Finally it was decided to replace it.

The erection of the 'new' tower of St Martin's Church was made possible by a legacy from Miss Anne Pedlar on condition that work started within ten years of her death. The chosen design came from Mr Sansom of Liskeard and the foundation stones were laid on 4 April 1900, by Dr W. Nettle (churchwarden), Mr S. Bone, Mr W.A. Jenkin (mayor) and Revd J. Norris (vicar).

The second largest church in Cornwall, fifteenth century St Martin's stands as a focal point of the town.

The interior of St Martin's Church with a glimpse of the organ which was removed in 1913. The canopy over the vicar's stall has yet to be positioned. The illumination is by gas light.

Castle Street leading out of the town to Plymouth. The high wall, now demolished once formed the garden boundary of Eliot House, 1897, the town residence of the Earls of St Germans. Since 1971 it has been the Lord Eliot Hotel. The houses on the left were demolished in a road widening scheme.

Castle Street and the junction of Higher Lux Street and Castle Lane in the 1920s. On the right the old Bull Post has been ousted by the cenotaph and opposite is the old school and a gas light with its lantern removed for summer cleaning at the council store in Well Lane. The vehicle is thought to be the Co-op delivery van.

Before the 'Ballot Act' of 1872, parliamentary hustings took place on the ground known today as Castle Park. This view from the 1930s shows the comparatively small trees which mark various royal coronations, together with their commemorative stones.

Two young ladies dressed to kill with spectacular hats and pinafores, taking a stroll while being admired by a group of young lads in the Castle Park in the early years of this century. The stone at the base of the tree in the foreground marks the coronation in 1902 of King Edward VII and Queen Alexandra.

Encircling a young beech tree, the famous wooden 'Round Seat' is remembered as a favourite meeting place for teenagers. This postcard is dated 1905. The tree, allegedly rotten and dangerous, was cut down in its maturity.

The Bull Stone, once used to tether bulls when cattle were sold on The Parade. Several 'coronation commemorative' stones figure in the background. The trees are now fully mature, as this picture dates from 1940.

These young girls, probably in their Sunday best, are enjoying the sunshine by the old Bull Post in the Castle Park. Also shown on the right is Mr Pooley's premises, furniture makers, undertakers and carpenters for several generations. Just visible on the extreme right are the flower gardens in front of the houses in Castle Street.

LISKEARD. LOWER CASTLE WALK.

Soon after the First World War the Bull Post was removed and the granite cenotaph to remember the town's fallen sons was erected in its place. Later the town 'lock-ups' at the left end of the park keeper's cottage were removed to make way for a private garage.

The corner of Greenbank Road and Pound Street and the main road to Plymouth. The sign is advising motorists to travel via Tavistock due to possible delays on the Torpoint ferry. The Tamar Road Bridge at Saltash had not yet been built. Some houses on the left have been demolished, as has the wall on the right. Today Barclays bank extension and car park is on the site. (Photograph from the John Rapson Collection).

Greenbank Chapel opened in May 1838 and due to the structural state of the building, closed at the end of August 1997.

Higher Lux Street: formerly St Luke's Street with Tonkins building on the right, and opposite Kilmar House, at one time a girls school, but now a residential home for the elderly.

At one time this was the entrance to Liskeard from the north. Today it is the lane which passes in front of the senior school. Some years ago a road widening scheme made a better approach to the town.

Liskeard, Belgrave Terrace.

The post is about to be delivered at Belgrave Terrace, Addington, near the turn of the century. The terraces and the garage on the opposite side have yet to be built. Note the old gas street lamp.

Russell Street Chapel, built on land acquired in 1853 by the Society of Protestant Dissenters Bible Christians, was closed in September 1958. It is now the home of the Liskeard Silver Band who purchased the property for £300.

An old view of Russell Street and Station Road. Some of the buildings on the left have been demolished. The large house on the right was once the residence of the gas company manager.

A general view of Victoria Terrace and The Nook in Station Road which is strangely free of traffic. The Nook, a turnpike house prior to that below the railway station, was demolished in the 1950s. Victoria Place stands on the site.

A rare aspect of Station Road taken from an upstairs window of The Nook during September 1940. Victoria Terrace is on the left and on the right is Ashpark Terrace, with Manley Terrace just making the scene.

Manley Terrace in the 1920s.

Manley Terrace, one of the Victorian terraces in Station Road which owes much to the prosperity associated with the mining boom in the mid-nineteenth century. On the left is the entrance to the Union Workhouse and on the right, the edge of what is now Rapsons Field car park.

The imposing entrance to Liskeard Union Workhouse, in Lamellion Street, now Station Road. The building was designed by Foulston during the 1830s. The archway has been demolished as has part of the central block with its bell turret. Wartime necessity claimed the railings. Today it is known as Lamellion Hospital. The hospital closed prior to the 2004 opening of the new Liskeard Community Hospital in Clemo Road.

Station Road and the copper beech trees outside the Union Workhouse with Manley Terrace beyond. Carwinion Terrace is hidden behind the trees in the foreground. In July 1872 according to The Cornish Times, a Mr Langmaid was making a desirable addition to Carwinion Terrace. The houses on the right have gone due to the construction of the town's by-pass.

An early view of Station Road and elegant Carwinion Terrace which was badly mauled when a number of its houses were demolished to make way for the town's by-pass in 1974 to 1975. Note the old gas street light.

Obviously a quiet period between trains, as this railwayman has time to chat with a passer-by or perhaps he is waiting for a coach to bring passengers for the next train down from the town. The cat is quite content to sit by the kerb. The Stag Hotel is on the left and Grove Park Terrace on the right.

Siskeard Railway Station.

What a contrast with today. When these passengers were about to depart for Plymouth there were porters to carry their luggage and see them settled in the train. The Brunel buildings at the end of the down platform were demolished in about 1980. The station building above the footbridge is now enclosed.

Always under threat of closure, the Liskeard to Looe branch line is used by countless tourists. By the look of the smoke and steam this locomotive is working hard on the steep climb from Coombe Junction into Liskeard during its hey-day in 1935.

Pencubitt House, was once the home of the Blamey family. During the war years it was a hostel for the Women's Land Army girls, between thirty and forty being based there. Today it is the Pencubitt Country House Hotel. In this photograph the frontage has been somewhat disfigured by the fire escapes.

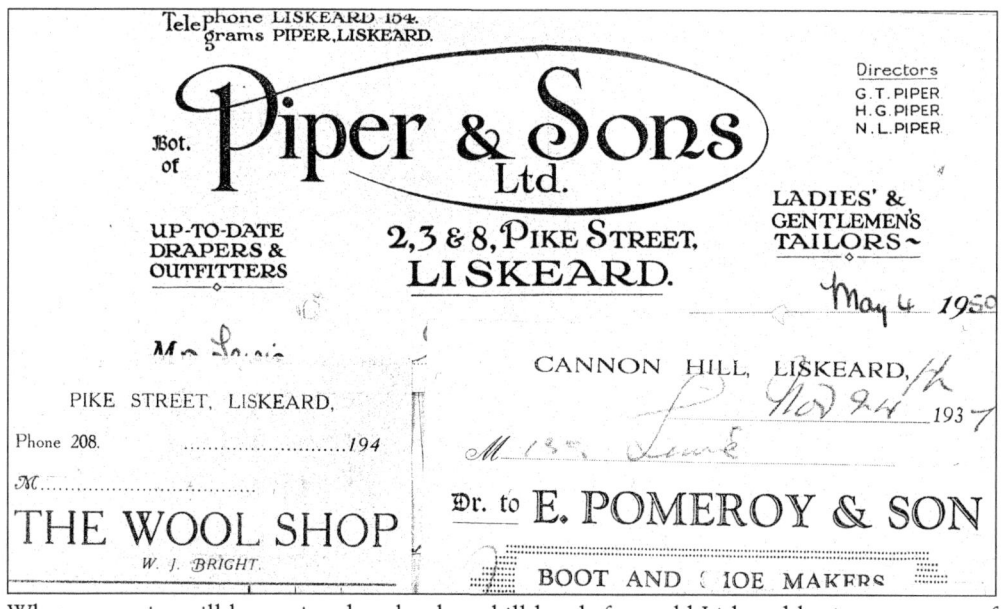

What memories will be conjured up by these bill heads from old Liskeard businesses, most of which have long ceased trading.

Tel. 2186.   No.

WILLIAM J. SWEET

Agricultural Engineer,
Shoeing and General Smith
DOCTOR'S LANE, POUND STREET,
LISKEARD

Welding, Wrought Ironwork		Agricultural Implement Repairs

Trailors and Gates made to order

$\mathcal{M}$rs. Lewis.   July 15   1955

J. L. PENGELLY & SON
FORE STREET, LISKEARD, CORNWALL
Telephone Liskeard 42124

22

C

To   *Mr Lewis 26 Park View –*

Date *January 13 73*

Tel N. 332

Y   868

W. H. SMITH & SON, L

NEWSAGENTS BOOKSELLERS STATIONERS LIBR
BOOKBINDERS PRINTERS AND ADVERTISING

W. H. SMITH & SON LTD
BOOKSELLERS, NEWSAGENTS & STATIONERS

COLLINGS & HICKS
T. C. HICKS, F.A.L.P.A., M.R.SAN.I.

Auctioneers, Surveyors, Estate Agents and Valuers

Valuations for all purposes.   All Classes of Insurance
Agents for Provincial Building Society

LISKEARD.   *14/4/1*

10, MARKET STREET, LISKEARD,

12th March 193 7

$\mathcal{M}$

Dr. to # B. & I. WHEELER,

STATIONERS

17353

EDGCUMBE, SON & COON
P. A.   LISKEARD   P. N.
Auctioneers & Valuers

Phone 2

INVOICE.   35

Phone: Liskeard 204

WESTERN SERVICE LISKEARD
H. E. D'ESTERRE.
GREENBANK ROAD, LISKEARD,
adio Trade Repairs. Wholesale Service Supplies.

Branch...................................... Date...........
Name................ *mrs Lewis*
Address................ *26 Park View*
BOUGHT OF THE

International
Tea
Co's **Stores Ltd.**
FAMOUS FOR FINE FOODS

9531   1

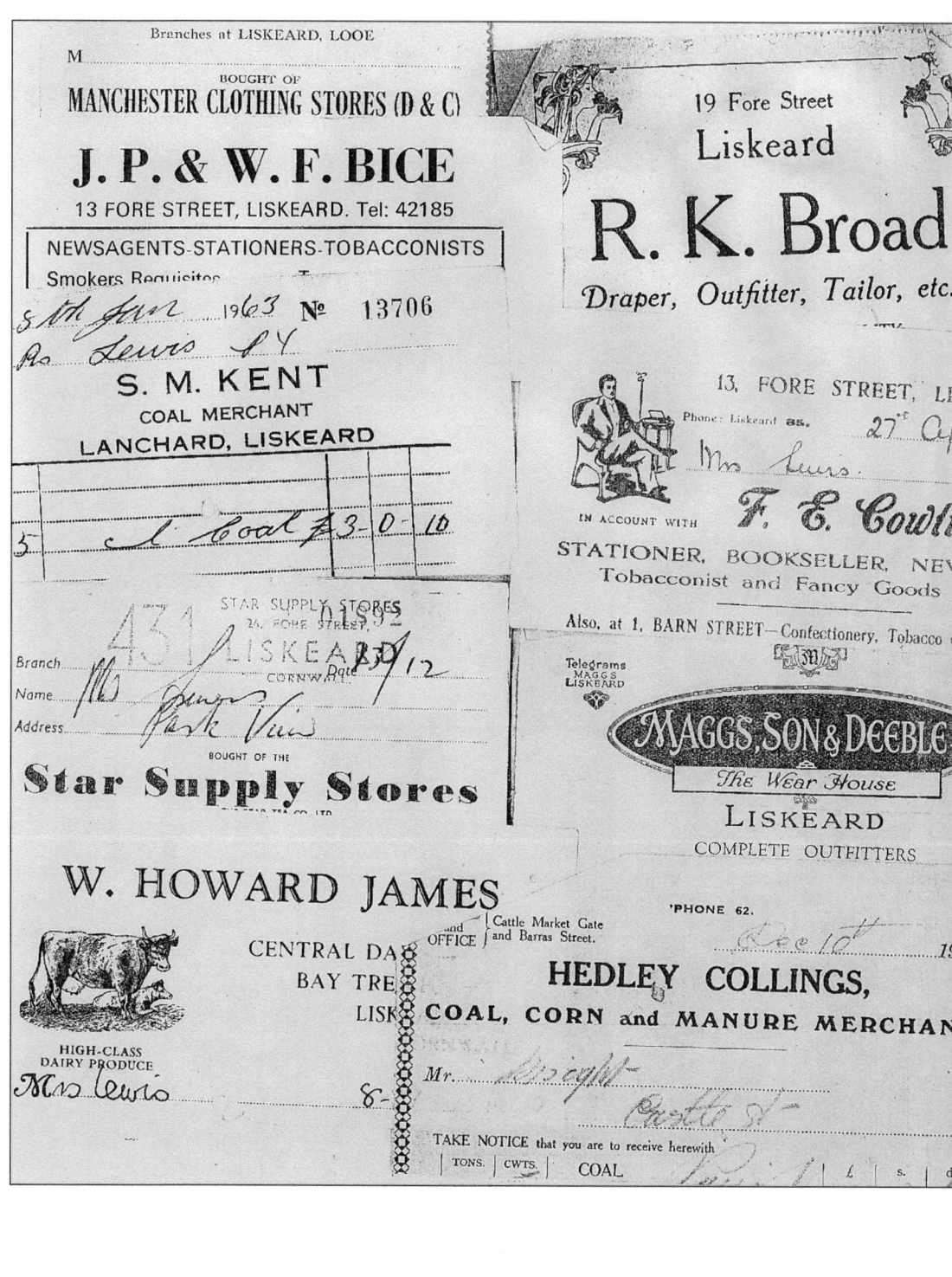

Branches at LISKEARD, LOOE

M

BOUGHT OF

MANCHESTER CLOTHING STORES (D & C)

J. P. & W. F. BICE

13 FORE STREET, LISKEARD. Tel: 42185

NEWSAGENTS-STATIONERS-TOBACCONISTS

Smokers Requisites

8th Jan 1963 № 13706

Re Lewis £4

S. M. KENT

COAL MERCHANT

LANCHARD, LISKEARD

5 1 Coal £3-0-10

A31

STAR SUPPLY STORES

24. FORE STREET,

LISKEARD

CORNWALL

01892

20/12

Branch

Name

Address Park View

BOUGHT OF THE

Star Supply Stores

THE STAR TEA CO. LTD.

19 Fore Street

Liskeard

R. K. Broad

Draper, Outfitter, Tailor, etc.

13, FORE STREET, LI

Phone : Liskeard 85.   27 Ap

Mrs Lewis.

IN ACCOUNT WITH   F. E. Cowli

STATIONER, BOOKSELLER, NEW
Tobacconist and Fancy Goods

Also, at 1. BARN STREET—Confectionery, Tobacco

Telegrams
MAGGS
LISKEARD

MAGGS, SON & DEEBLE

The Wear House

LISKEARD

COMPLETE OUTFITTERS

W. HOWARD JAMES

CENTRAL DA

BAY TRE

LISK

HIGH-CLASS
DAIRY PRODUCE

Mrs Lewis   8-

and   Cattle Market Gate
OFFICE and Barras Street.

'PHONE 62.

Dec 10th   19

HEDLEY COLLINGS,

COAL, CORN and MANURE MERCHAN

Mr. Wright

Castle St

TAKE NOTICE that you are to receive herewith

TONS.	CWTS.	COAL		£	s.	d

Two

Liskeard
People on Parade

Over the generations Liskeard people have made their marks both at home and abroad. This chapter depicts a small selection of some who have held public office within the town and others who have gone about their daily lives in a quieter way: all have one thing in common, they have, each in his or her own way, added to the pot-pourri that is life in a small east Cornwall market town.

A group of Liskeard Old Cornwall Society members during a 'Pilgrimage' to Goon Vean China Clay works near St Austell in 1958. Among those identified are: Mr and Mrs Matheson, Miss Ivy Coath, Mrs Coath, Mrs Taylor and Mr D. Lewis.

A group photographed in Lower Lux Street, in the 1950s, who are about to embark on an excursion. They are thought to be patrons of the Red Lion Inn which is on the right, one of the oldest public houses in the town.

Patrons of the 'Tap Room Bar', part of the Webb's Hotel complex, prior to one of their outings, c. 1935. Today the former bar is a hair dressing salon.

The Wesleyan Guild attached to the chapel was a popular organisation in the town. Members used to enjoy occasional 'rambles' and in 1928 one took them to Watergate Bay, near Looe. Among those identified are, Mrs M. Lewis, Miss Barratt, Miss Mildred Matthew, Arthur Broad, Leslie Piper and Miss Flossie Prescott.

Members of the Wesleyan Guild letting their hair down and having a thoroughly good time in 1928. Some of those pictured are Miss Flossie Prescott, Miss Hunkin, Miss Barratt, Mrs Lewis, Miss Mildred Matthew, Leslie Piper and Arthur Broad.

An attractive portrait of Leading Firewoman Instructor and dispatch rider Miss Yvonne Lewis wearing her wartime fire-service uniform.

Mr Huddy, the mayor with a gathering of dignitaries on The Parade. Although the exact occasion is uncertain it has been suggested that it dates from September 1909 when five firemen were presented with twenty year, long service medals after a mock fire exercise at Webb's Hotel. The gentleman standing in the front wearing the cap is Mr Richard Bright.

Mr John Ugalde of Liskeard receiving his twenty and a half year Long Service and Good Conduct Medal from Her Majesty's Chief Inspector of Fire Services H.M. Smith Esq CBE MI Fire E on the occasion of the opening of the new fire station at Launceston on 15 November 1958.

A group of Liskeard firemen pictured in November 1967 on the occasion when the fire station received a new appliance. Among those pictured are: R. Collings, J. Collings, R. Ugalde, E. Collins, W. Moore, B. Rowe, L. Davey, W. Kurn, J. Snell, S. Quiller and F. Hocking.

Liskeard firemen posed for this picture in June 1977, when Station Officer Snell presented Leading Fireman A. Gwillam with a watch to mark his fifteen years service.

Mr Douglas Lewis, assistant organist at St Martin's Parish Church from 1947-1971, pictured at the console of the old organ. (Photograph from the John Rapson Collection).

St Martin's Church choir outside the tower entrance in the early 1950s. Among those pictured are Canon J. Parsons, Mr Arthur Andrew, organist, church wardens Mr Edward Brown, (headmaster of the church school) and Mr Stuart Matheson, Mr Cyril Bunn and Mr Clogg. Three members of one family are pictured: Mr Tom Pickard, tenor, Mrs Pickard and their son who is among the boys.

Church choir members taking a break during a recording session at St Martin's Church in the 1950s. The recording was made for a double wedding, the Misses Andrew whose marriages were to take place simultaneously hundreds of miles apart, using the same order of service and music; the one in Liskeard the other in the Middle East, where the bridegroom worked for an oil company.

The crowning of the Temperance Queen at Trewithen House in 1951. Among those identified are: Queen Molly Chaston, Barbara Williams, Lewella Britt, Margaret Hawken, Marion Day, Iris Crocker, Susan Evans, Sandra Preston, Dorothy Crocker, Anne Bailey, Christopher Day and Geoffrey Bailey.

The crowning of the Temperance Queen in 1953. (Photograph from the John Rapson Collection.)

The Liskeard Temperance Brass and Reed Band; prominent in the front row is bandmaster, Mr James Mitchell.

Liskeard Silver Band pictured in 1928 when they were among the prize winners at Stenalees Band Contest. The young man in the back row on the right was Addis Bailey then aged about twelve years. Others shown are: R.J. Bray, D. Herring, H. Edgecumbe, W. Colmer, S. Cummine, C. Tickell, W.J. Herring, A. Davey, B. Hosmin, J. Edmunds, J. Ugalde, H. Doney, W. Herring, L. Jones, N. Mallett hon. sec. in lounge suit, T. Priest, bandmaster and A. Phillips.

Members of Liskeard Drama Group in Dickensian costume entertaining customers at Kernow Mill during the run-up to Christmas 1992.

Miss Hitchens Gladilova School of Dancing put on annual shows for a number of years. This is a group of her pupils shown in 1957-1958.

This attractive gypsy couple, Miss Yvonne Lewis and Miss Phyllis Symons, formed part of the carnival procession in 1935. Speculation was evident among the on-lookers as to the identity of the young man.

Carnival time in Liskeard. This Lyons Tea float appeared in the procession in 1926. Miss Yvonne Lewis is the young lady wearing the large hat.

First prize for the best decorated vehicle in the carnival was won in 1935 by Mrs Roseveare and Mrs Hooper.

A happy group of Women's Land Army girls in the Liskeard carnival procession in 1944. It's smiles all round as their topical tableau, 'Grow More Food' complete with a real live lamb had just been awarded first and special prize.

Her Majesty the Queen in Liskeard in May 1956. Here she is seen on The Parade speaking with civic dignitaries including the Mayor Mr Arthur Snell, Alderman Spurway, Councillors: Westlake, C.M. Dennis, Mr Douglas Marshall MP for the Bodmin Division, Canon Parsons, Vicar of Liskeard, mace bearer Mr E.G. Northcott and the Chairman of the District Council.

Her Royal Highness, Princess Margaret speaking with Girls Brigade members in June 1973. (Photograph from the John Rapson Collection.) Also shown is Mr John Goldsworthy, the last borough mayor.

These youngsters chatting to Her Royal Highness Princess Margaret appear to be enjoying the royal occasion in 1973. (Photograph from the John Rapson Collection.)

Her Royal Highness Princess Margaret shares a joke with the Scout troop in 1973. (Photograph from the John Rapson Collection.)

The Mayor and Mayoress of Liskeard, Mr and Mrs J. Howarth receiving their chains of office at the Mayor Choosing ceremony in May 1967. Their first official engagement was in Plymouth when they were among those who welcomed Francis Chichester after his epic voyage round the world aboard his yacht Gypsy Moth IV.

The Mayor and Mayoress of Liskeard Mr and Mrs. J. Howarth in procession with civic dignitaries in Pound Street in May 1967. Pictured are: Alderman George Maddaver, Canon Deryck Davey, and mace bearer Mr E. Northcott.

Mr and Mrs J. Howarth, mayor and mayoress, seen here in 1967, distributing 'buns' an old Liskeard custom which they revived after many years.

These youngsters seem somewhat overawed by the occasion as they receive their 'buns' from the mayor and mayoress, Mr and Mrs J. Howarth in 1967. Sadly the custom seems to have lapsed again.

A part of the mayor's duties is to present prizes at the local agricultural show. Here the mayor and mayoress, Mr and Mrs J. Howarth, are seen with show officials. Pictured on the extreme right is Mr Jock Stanier, Duchy of Cornwall Land Agent. (Photograph from the John Rapson Collection.)

Miss Yvonne Lewis and Miss Audrey Clark with prize winning Great Danes, Jason and Juno at the Liskeard Agricultural Show in 1969.

Miss Yvonne Lewis with Gussie her prize winning home bred sow at the Liskeard Agricultural Show.

A happy band of Women's Land Army girls photographed at Pencubitt in 1944.

Mrs Christine Pampling setting off for the wards at Lamellion Hospital with a well laden Red Cross trolley shop.

The Mayor and Mayoress of Liskeard, Mr and Mrs N. Pampling, pictured here in 1985 with a special visitor to the town, Monsieur Jacques Charter the Mayor of Quimperle, Brittany, Liskeard's twin town.

Smiling faces at a street party at Lanchard to celebrate the Queen's Silver Jubilee in 1977.

One of several street parties held in Liskeard to mark VE Day 1945. This well attended party was held at Manley Terrace in Station Road.

An unusual photograph of the women's ward at Passmore Edwards Hospital, decorated for a special occasion. The contrast between the nurses' uniforms then as opposed to now is interesting. Stiff white caps, starched white aprons, puffed sleeves and white cuffs were the norm. One wonders—who was the patient? Who were the nurses?

A happy group after a tree planting ceremony, at Addington to mark seventy-five years of Girl Guides in Liskeard. The town's oldest Guide, at that time, Miss Hitchins had the honour during June 1985.

Liskeard Scouts on the occasion of the first turf being cut for the site of their new hut in the 1960s.

Members of the Liskeard Rotary Club who presented Liskeard Scouts with a cheque for £100 towards their building fund in 1965. Among those identified are Ian Busbridge, Jack Gillbard, Ken Julian and John Jackson. (Photograph from the John Rapson Collection.)

All eyes are on the cheque for £100 presented to the Scouts by representatives of the town's Rotary Club in 1965. (Photograph from the John Rapson Collection.)

A scene from the Liskeard Scouts Gang Show in 1976. (Photograph from the John Rapson Collection.)

Miss Martha Rapson and a group of her pupils photographed in the 1920s at Highwood House, her private school which she opened in 1899 and conducted for fifty-four years. It is estimated that she taught between 2,000 and 3,000 pupils. Miss Rapson died in 1957.

Photograph taken in the Castle Park showing Miss Yvonne Lewis proudly wearing the uniform of Miss Martha Rapson's school, 1928.

A well posed group of pupils at Varley Lane School in 1928. The teachers were Mr N.T. Jaco, headmaster and assistant master Mr J. Hunkin.

Pupils at Varley Lane School in the mid-1930s.

Where are they now? These youngsters attended Liskeard Council School in 1932-1933.

These pupils attended Liskeard Junior School in the late 1950s. Among those identified are: Phillip Toms, Malcolm Sharpe, Sandra Roberts, Graham Warbutton, Delia Gimblett, Linda Hoskins, Sandra Pound and Jeanette Kern.

Above left: Mr Arthur Roseveare will be remembered by many as groundsman at Lux Park Cricket Field. He also drove the Western National Buses and in his spare time he repaired bicycles. Above right: Mr Arthur Roseveare, Mrs Ruth Laity and Mrs Ada Roseveare. The Austin Standard car was registered JY 108 and cost about £130 in the late 1940s.

Liskeard Football Club in 1902. The line-up was Libby, A. Craddick, G. Craddick, Penwarden, Trueman, Bray, Quiller, Blamey, Bartlett, Hosking and Vosper.

Liskeard football team in 1904-05. Team members were, W. Welsh, C. Jenkins, A. Prior, F. Libby, G. Craddick, C. Blamey, H. Volk, F. Richards, A.Craddick, K. Blamey, S. Pearce.

In 1906 Liskeard Reserves were the winners of the Eastern Division and Cornwall Junior Cups. The team were P. Bond, F. Roberts, H. Collings, E. Coles, T. Hooper, A. Bray, C. Coath, C. Whitford, Richardson, G. Lyne, P. Symons.

In May 1923 Liskeard Reserves shared the Isaac Foot Shield with Polperro. Members of the team were: H. Vennard, R. Collings, C. Repper, Capt R. Salter, J. Govett, H. Lidstone, L. Carne, J. Denis, T. Wilson, S. Sleep, C. Martin, W. Carne, R. Botterell (Hon League Sec).

Liskeard Reserves 1926-1927. These were Curtis, Quiller, Pearce, Grigg, Blackwell, Wyatt, Reeves, Taylor, Craddick, Bidgood, Davey, Bray, Hill, Wills, Lukey and Tonkin.

Liskeard AFC 1947-48. Team members include: N. Pearce, B. Westlake, H. Dawe, H. Rickard, J. Pink, J. Jane, R. Crocker, J. Crocker, G. Cumine, G. Cowling, J. Bedford, W. Hoskin, R. Hooper.

The Liskeard Cricket Team of 1912. Among those pictured are: T. Gundry, B. Rowe, G. Lyne, F. Cowling, G. Evely, J. Isaac, R. Thomas, F. Forse, P. Dingle, W. Hooper, W. Hoskin, P. Pond, E. Tindall, A. Rogers, E. Cooper, B. Stephens, N. Hambly.

In 1951 the Liskeard Cricket Club line up was: B. Gudmunsen, G. Bickford, E. O'Brien, A. Bersey, W. Hoskin, W. Till, D. Challis, E. Brown, (umpire) T. Phipps, St L. Stephens, Miss O'Brien, (scorer) H. Taylor, R. Marchant, and R. Harris, (financial secretary).

Three

St Keyne to Duloe

This chapter covers the acres sandwiched between the West Looe and East Looe rivers. The land hereabouts is generally less harsh and changes have taken place in the villages as the holiday industry encroaches.

St Keyne Church.

St Keyne Church, looking east.

Patience is a virtue, as these horses undoubtedly found waiting patiently outside Landers Corn Mill at St Keyne.

Duloe has grown a lot since this photograph was taken. It is just possible to see the ancient stone circle in the top right hand corner of the picture.

St Cuby's church at Duloe in the days when it was lit by oil lamps.

The Post Office at Duloe in Edwardian times. Unfortunately neither the post mark or the sender's name of this postcard are legible. Arrangements are being made with the Misses Moor of Little Larnick Duloe for a meeting at noon on the following Thursday on Looe Bridge, some six miles away.

High fashion, particularly in the millinery stakes, seems to be the order of the day among the ladies of Duloe Band of Hope in the early 1900s. What must hats like these have cost at that time and what would be the equivalent cost today?

There is scarcely a smile among this group of Duloe School pupils in about 1900. Perhaps teacher has laid down the law and is watching closely. Young Edgar Crapp, third from the left in the front row is the only one identified.

Mr Edgar Crapp, second on left in the back row with a group of his chums during the First World War. The majority perished in the conflict. The dog survived.

Mr and Mrs Norman Woodman with Canon W.G. Steer of Launceston posing for photographs after their marriage at Duloe Church on Easter Monday, 1952. Canon Steer, one time Rector at Duloe, returned to officiate at the ceremony. By all accounts it rained in the morning and as a result poor Auntie Gladys slipped on the church step.

Duloe AFC Fete in the early 1950s. This line-up shows the ladies team for the day, who played against the men, Duloe Blues. Among those identified are Molly Rounsevell, Barbara Woodman, Christine Woodman, Kay Kettlety, Ruby Rogers, Joan Woodley and Joan Vowler. Apparently the result is best forgotten.

Four

Moorswater
to Dobwalls

Moorswater, once squeezed between the headwaters of the Looe Liskeard Canal and the rail line from the mines of Caradon Hill has, as a village, almost disappeared. Only a few buildings and the viaduct remain to jog the memory about what was once a busy area and Dobwalls has been sliced in two by the A38 trunk road. In recent years the Dobwalls by-pass road has been opened and vehicular traffic through the village has been greatly reduced.

A corner of Lamellion hamlet in the early years of this century.

The majestic wooden trestle Brunel viaduct of 1859 at Moorswater, sweeping across the valley on fourteen stately piers with the stone piers of the new viaduct beginning to dominate the scene.

Moorswater Viaduct

1905

A general view of Moorswater in 1905. The stone viaduct has been built but down below horse-drawn traffic still holds sway.

An 'up train' slowly crosses Moorswater Viaduct. The Brunel piers have been reduced in height probably for safety reasons. Shortly after this photograph was taken steam hauled trains began to disappear. The Cornish Times reported on 25 April 1958 that the first hydraulic diesel locomotive to come into regular service between Plymouth and Penzance had passed through Liskeard station.

Once on the main highway, the old toll house at Looe Mills dates from 1837. Today it has been side tracked and is scarcely noticed as vehicular traffic hurtles along the A38 trunk road.

Moorswater Football Team were the group leaders in the Cornwall Junior Cup in the 1928-1929 season. The line up was R. Hooper, G. Harper, F. Hobbs, W. Dawe, F. Saunders, J. Deeble, P. Bray, H. Dawe, W. Hoskin, J. Metters and L.P. Dawe.

Moorswater fielded this formidable line-up in the Liskeard and District League in 1929-1930, football season. The team includes: G.Harper, M. Scoble, M. McCormick, F. Hobbs, G. Redler, J. Gay, E. Hynes, W. Dawe, P. Dawe, R. Harper, H. Dawe, W. Hoskin, C. Wilson and R. Hooper.

Moorswater Football Team in 1944. The players were: R. Symons, G. Netherton, A. Stone, J. Bidgood, D. Tamblyn, J. Williams, W. Mitchell, R. Lyneham, K. Crago, R. Crago, H. Dawe, D. Dobson, W. Dawe.

This group of players of Moorswater Football Team in 1946-47. The group inludes: C. Tozer, A. Copplestone, W. Dawe, H. Rickard, H. Dawe, W. Lobb, W.H. Mitchell, G. Hancock, J. Pink, S. Clarke, V. Trebilcock, A. Evans, W. Hoskin, G.O. Cowling, W. Bailey, R. Crocker, M. Scoble.

A corner of Dobwalls village when life was much slower. Horses reigned supreme and the now ubiquitous motor car was then still a curiosity.

Dobwalls village before the installation of the traffic lights on the junction with the Bodmin, St Austell and Liskeard Roads. The nightmare of Dobwalls Hill has been eased by the one way traffic system which comes into operation on summer weekends. Much of the new development is away from the main road.

Above left: 'Vera' from Yorkshire, who was among a work detail of Women's Land Army girls to Bokenna Farm at Dobwalls. It was here that she met and later married the farmer's son, John Hoskins. To this day Mrs Hoskins remembers cutting kale with icicles several inches long hanging from the leaves during the bitter winter of 1944. Above right: From their hostel at Pencubitt the girls were transported to the various farms in the back of an army lorry, often singing as they went. They were dropped off in small groups depending on the job to be done.

A group of Women's Land Army girls on Charlie Ferris's farm at Lansallos in 1944.

By 1944, 80,000 women had joined the Land Army. Most came from the large cities. Hay making, lifting potatoes and milking cows were among the more pleasant jobs. Sheep dipping physically upset some girls. On the wider war front the 'D-day' landings had taken place in June.

Land Army girls had seven days official leave a year. Tractor driving was something in which they soon became accomplished. Eating 'croust' in the hayfield was a welcome diversion. On the home front twenty-five per cent of fresh eggs were produced by domestic hen keepers.

This happy-go-lucky band of Women's Land Army girls, Peggy, Dot, Bunney, Jean, Vera and Nelly seem to be enjoying themselves after a heavy fall of snow at Pencubitt in 1944. How did the photographer fair? All the snowballs seem to be aimed at the camera.

Five

St Neot to Warleggan

These two villages both clasp the southern edge of Bodmin Moor. Of the two, St Neot is probably the best known, resting in its hollow but much changed after the attentions of the developer, while Warleggan is luckily to some extent still remote and little known.

Photographed soon after the turn of the century these youngsters, fascinated by the camera, are taking a rest on Goonzion Downs. St Neot village nestles down in the valley.

The Village, St.. Neot

An early view of St Neot, then a small quiet edge of Bodmin Moor community and long before it was 'discovered' by the developers, seen from the windy heights of Goonzion Downs.

The Bridge, St. Neot

A picturesque corner of old St Neot, where the bridge spans the River Loveny which rises near Bolventor on Bodmin Moor. A piece of history is revealed by the sign, Carlyon Club on the building. Note the old petrol pump.

An unusual view of St Neot Church and Vicarage from the gardens.

St Neot Vicarage with the then open view to Goonzion in the 1930s. Is that the vicar hard at work in the garden ?

St Neot Church from the south east.

The interior of St Neot Church, note the old hanging oil lamps. The fifteenth century stained glass windows restored in the nineteenth century tell of the legends of St Neot and are among the finest in the country.

A familiar scene at St Neot in the early 1900s, was Mr Lawry standing outside his blacksmiths shop waiting for a local farmer to bring his horse to be shod. Today the building is the Old Smithy Tea Rooms.

A flock of sheep would cause chaos in the main street of St Neot today. This photograph dates from the early twentieth century.

Local men carrying the oak branch to the church at St Neot in the early 1950s. It was here that it adorned the tower to mark Oak Apple Day, on 29 May, when King Charles II, hid in an oak tree after the Battle of Worcester. Among those identified are: Bevil Bunt, John Cawrse, Eric Bunt, Russell Rowe and Joe Bunt.

The popular Half Way Inn between Liskeard and Bodmin as it was just prior to the outbreak of the Second World War.

St Bartholomew's Church at Warleggan, where the Revd W. Densham lost all his congregation and rather than preach to an empty church, he placed cardboard figures inscribed with the names of the absentee parishioners in the pews and carried on preaching Sunday after Sunday.

A peaceful corner of Warleggan village.

Warleggan village seems lost to the world in this photograph and even today it is remote and mysterious.

Trengoffe Manor, Warleggan which was burnt down in January 1969.

Six

Pensilva, Minions and Upton Cross

Pensilva began life as a small mining settlement which has expanded rapidly over the last decades. Minions, formerly known as Cheesewring village, is the highest village in Cornwall and stands amid the rugged granite-strewn face of Bodmin Moor while not far away in more agricultural land rests Upton Cross.

A general view of Pensilva in the days when it was a scattered mining community.

Bygone Pensilva, growing now but still centred round the local chapel.

An almost deserted Princess Road, Pensilva, with its rows of small cottages built to house miners and their families. The motor vehicle probably belongs to the photographer and the model, a companion, as the 'poser' appears in several photographs around this time.

FORE STREET, PENSILVA.

94809 (V)

This old picture of Fore Street, Pensilva, shows what the village, largely dependant on the prosperity of the local mines during the nineteenth century was like, up until the outbreak of the First World War.

The Cross, Pensilva, Looking West.

The Cross at Pensilva before the days of the motor car when it was safe to stand in the road. Today it is drastically changed, it is a busy road junction with a plethora of road signs and a car passing by at what seems every minute.

An early view of Princess Road, Pensilva. Everybody seems to be wearing their best bib and tucker for the camera.

A turn of the century view from Pensilva long before it was developed and there was a clear view toward Callington. Note the bicycle and horse-drawn traffic.

A quiet corner of Pensilva with the distant view toward Callington and Kit Hill, with its stack on the summit.

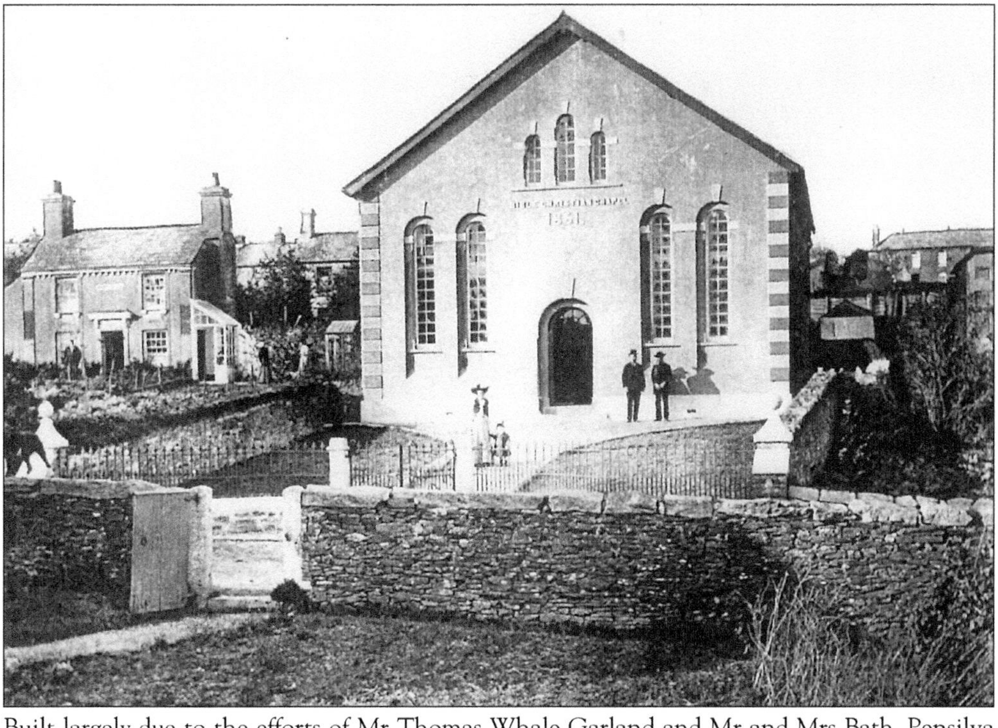

Built largely due to the efforts of Mr Thomas Whale Garland and Mr and Mrs Bath, Pensilva Bible Christian Chapel was opened on St Valentine's Day in 1861. On the first Sunday following, the building was packed with worshippers.

An early view of Cheesewring village (Minions) in the early 1900s, showing the extensive use of granite in the buildings. The centre building was at one time a general store and filling station kept my Mrs 'Flo' Benfell. Today it is a restaurant and tea-rooms known as Hurlers Halt.

Cheesewring village, now known as Minions. Note the horse-drawn vehicles lined up outside Gerry's Cheesewring Hotel.

During its hey-day Phoenix United Mine at Caradon was one of the most successful producers of copper and tin in Cornwall. It closed down in 1898 but reopened in 1907 and two years later received a visit from King George V and Queen Mary when a new digging was named The Prince of Wales Shaft. The mine was finally abandoned in 1914.

South Phoenix Mine, Cheesewring, Near Liskeard.

The vast quantities of copper and tin raised from the South Phoenix Mine complex are legendary. In October 1872 a new engine having a second cylinder was erected and successfully set to work by Mr Loam of Liskeard. Also in the same year The Cornish Times reported that for the first time a surgeon was based in the vicinity due to the growing number of miners and their families in the area. Previously the nearest surgeon was located in Liskeard.

A fine bunch of workers taking a hard earned break at the Cheesewring granite quarry which opened in the 1800s. Note the dogs and the jaunty angles of the headgear. The Health and Safety Executive would have a field day as what appears to be a box of explosives is much in evidence. Now long closed, the quarry is a mecca for rock climbers.

Cheesewring Quarry as it was in the 1960s. The rail lines over which the trains travelled to convey the granite to Moorswater are still in situ.

The long approach to Cheesewring Quarry, probably much as the old quarry workers would have seen it.

The Cheesewring appears dangerously close to the quarry rim. Today the natural rock formation is on the visitors' trail from the Minions Heritage Centre.

Duchy Terrace, Upton Cross, around the turn of the century. The occasion is unknown but these youngsters are all dressed in their Sunday best. Caps are the order of the day for the boys.

The chapel at Upton Cross dates from 1864. Standing next to it is the post office, later a private dwelling and today the village shop and post office once again. Note the old motor-cycle and side-car by the chapel gate.

Seven

Menheniot

Menheniot is about two parish strides away from the Cornish borderland parishes and covers an area of mainly agricultural land of small farms set amid folding hills between which run rivers and streams. This chapter shows something of the Menheniot in the years gone by.

The Menheniot of over eighty years ago was much more laid back than it is today; these old boys appear to have all the time in the world to chat and receive mail from the postman who has probably walked out from Liskeard.

In the years before the First World War horse-drawn traffic in and around Menheniot was an every day sight. This group is probably going to the local smithy.

An early view of St Lalluwys Church at Menheniot, taken by a local man named Harris at around the turn of the century.

The view of Menheniot Church as it was in the earlier years of the century.

Interior of Menheniot Church, showing the old oil lamps and the memorial to William Holwell Carr, absentee vicar of the parish who paid a curate to live here and conduct church services and other parish business in the eighteenth century. Carr himself travelled the world buying paintings and when he died he bequeathed them to the National Gallery, which was then in its infancy.

Menheniot in more recent times. In 1969 The Cornish Guardian reported that after seventeen years discussion it was decided at a public meeting to have thirteen street lamps in the parish at a cost of £440. This figure put 6d (2½p) on the rates. The nearby road stone quarry, opened before the First World War, closed in November 1969.

Coldrenick House at Menheniot was built in 1862 for the Sneyd family. It was a timber frame construction with brick in-fill while the interior walls were of cowhair, plaster and boarding. Its colour scheme varied between pink and white or black and white. Eventually it became a liability as it was often in need of costly maintenance so it was finally demolished in 1966.

116

Eight

St Cleer, Darite
Tremar, Commonmoor
Crows Nest

This chapter mainly concerns itself with the smattering of villages which sprang up during the nineteenth century mining boom. Once a hard working area of mines and quarries, the relics of which still scatter the landscape, today it is largely a dormitory area for Liskeard, Launceston, Bodmin and places farther afield.

St Cleer Church dominates the older part of the village which suddenly expanded after copper and tin was discovered in the area.

The spacious interior of St Cleer Church in the days when it had yet to be converted to electric lighting.

A quiet corner of St Cleer around the turn of the century.

These youngsters lived at St Cleer in the days of the mining boom. Note the mine chimneys dotting the horizon and landscape.

One of the lesser roads through St Cleer. The bullock has strayed into the village from off the moors and is satisfying its curiosity.

Photographed during the First World War these St Cleer men were part of The Duke Of Cornwall's Light Infantry Volunteers. Among those shown are: C. Pomeroy, F. Edwards, F. Cock, E. Avery, ? Mitchell, A. Roberts, S. Stephens, ? Hooper, N. Cock, H. Freeman, C. Goss and W.J. Hoskin.

Miss Hill planting a double flowering pink cherry tree next to the Holy Well. It was a gift to St Cleer village from Miss Hill to mark Her Majesty the Queen's Silver Jubilee in 1977.

Local youngsters giving a display of maypole dancing at St Cleer Primary School centenary celebrations in 1977.

St Cleer Cricket Club after winning the Skentelbery Cup against Lostwithiel in 1922. Among team members identified are: E. Pollard, Revd Hayton, W. Williams, F. Stephens, Lord Fortescue, S. Stephens, S. Skentelbery, E.J. Avery, C. Pascoe, N. Nicholas, W. Hoskin, Capt J. Acland, T. Cock, G. James, G. Williams and Mr Kirk-Bullock, (umpire).

St Cleer Cricket Club, 1926. Players were: A. Clogg, R. Stephens, H. James, W. Hoskin, W.J. Hoskin, E. Gibson, F. Stephens, S. Stephens, W. Williams, Mrs Stephens and J. Angear.

St Cleer Football Team. In the 1932-33 line up were H. Rennie, C. Goss, G. Harper, A.Tonkin, R. Retallick, N. Reeves, L. Skentelbery, W. Hillson, J. Farran, C. Cowling, J. Cock, R. Harper, R. Hall, W. Hoskin, J.Cock and C.Wilson.

This part of Bodmin Moor under Tregarrack Tor was flooded by the East Cornwall Water Board to form the Sibley Back Reservoir in 1969. The lake, which holds 700 million gallons of water when full to capacity, was made by damming the Sibley Back Brook, a tributary of the River Fowey. It covers an area of 140 acres.

The start of excavations for the Sibley Back Reservoir Dam which is 750 feet long and 70 feet high. It was opened in June 1969 by Sir John Carew Pole and later dedicated by the Rt Revd J.M. Key, Bishop of Truro.

An early view of Tremar Coombe before it was developed.

Tremar village in the 1920s, before the real building boom. Today's rush of vehicular traffic would ensure that the chicken would never make stately progress across the road.

TREMAR WIN THE 1938 LEAGUE SHIELD.

Tremar Village football team who won the Isaac Foot Shield against Downderry in 1938. The match was played at Lux Park, Liskeard. The line up was W. Harvey, R. Webb, F. Sanders, K. Crocker, S. Stephens, T. Newman, J. Watkins, M. Doney, G. Hancock, R. Crocker, C. Hall, R. Cornish, C. Wilson, C. Cowling, R. Cook, W. Hoskin, (insert photograph) who did not play due to illness.

Looking towards the scattered edge of the Bodmin Moor village of Railway Terrace, now called Darite, which sprang up as a result of all the prospecting activity around Caradon Hill in the nineteenth century.

High summer soon after the hay harvest, looking across the fields to Darite, August 1926.

COMMON MOOR NEAR LISKEARD   C.229

Commonmoor, once known as Pilla Moor, came into being as a result of the mining activity in the area. The Brake, a complex of bungalows has yet to be built on the land in the centre of the photograph.

Rose Cottages, Commonmoor, from the air.

An early view of Crows Nest village in the days when the passing of motor vehicles was an event; even the dog feels that it is quite safe to lie in the roadway.

Obviously a special but unidentified occasion at Crows Nest Chapel in the early years of this century. After 124 years the chapel was closed in 1965 and has since been demolished.

535 DRAYNES BRIDGE IN WINTER. RIVER FOWEY, REDGATE, NEAR LISKEARD

A fall of snow adds its own particular enchantment to this scene of Dreynes Bridge on the River Fowey. A visitors' car park now occupies the land adjoining the building.